PRIMARY 1

MUSIC

BY ME

AUTHORS:
Fernando Fernández Picos
Álvaro Fernández Rodríguez
Mª Estrella Rodríguez López
Lucía González Hevia

LANGUAGE CONSULTANT:

CONTENTS

Unit	Page	LISTEN	DISCOVER
1. HOUSE OF SOUNDS	4	• Nice and bad sounds	• Long and short sounds • Beats
2. SONGS AT SCHOOL	12	• Loud and soft sounds	• One beat: *Ta* • Sounds and silences
3. STREET BEATS	20	• High and low sounds	• Repeat with me • Create your rhythm
4. SHOP AND SING	28	• Timbre	• *Ti ti* • What sounds do they make?
5. MUSICAL LANDSCAPES	36	• Natural and artificial sounds	• *Ta-a* • Notes do, re and mi
6. SHOWTIME!	44	• Volume and speed	• Notes fa and sol • The stave and treble clef
TERM 1	52	**Technology in Music:** Listening to music **In tune:** How do we communicate?	
TERM 2	54	**Technology in Music:** Music around us **In tune:** Listen safely and responsibly	
TERM 3	56	**Technology in Music:** Playing music **In tune:** Feel the music	
FESTIVALS	58	Christmas is here! The Easter bunny Summer is here!	
SONG LYRICS	64		
PICTURE DICTIONARY	70		

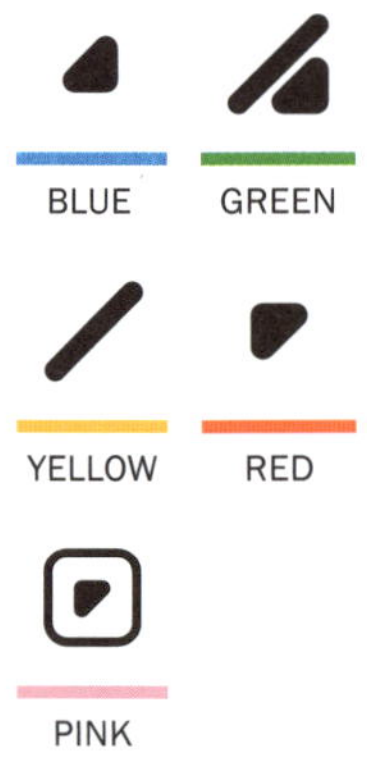

PLAY	SING	DANCE/CREATE	TALK ABOUT MUSIC
• Body percussion	• Our voice	• **Dance:** *In my kitchen*	• Types of sound (nice, bad, long, short) • Clap your hands. / Stamp your feet. / Pat your legs
• Feel the rhythm	• Parts of a song	• **Create:** Hawaiian rhythm sticks	• Types of sound (loud, soft) • Chorus / verse • My favourite song
• Wooden percussion	• Breathing	• **Dance:** *In the street*	• Wooden percussion instruments • Types of sound (high, low) • Yes, it is. / No, it isn't.
• Metal percussion	• Who's singing?	• **Create:** Maracas	• Percussion instruments • My favourite percussion instrument.
• Drums and more	• Musical scale	• **Dance:** The pretty flower dance	• Types of sound (natural, artificial) • Yes, I can. / No, I can't.
• Playing with rhythm	• *Follow the robot*	• **Create:** A concert programme	• Names of professions related to music • Notes (do, re, mi, fa, sol) • My concert programme

1 HOUSE OF SOUNDS

2 Listen and sing.

In my kitchen

In my kitchen, in my kitchen,
in my kitchen, I hear sounds.
In my kitchen, in my kitchen,
in my kitchen, I hear sounds.

...

p. 64

1. **Circle four objects that produce sounds in the song.**
2. **Are there more objects in the picture that can make sounds?**
3. **What shapes can you see in the picture?**

Listen

NICE AND BAD SOUNDS

Sounds can be nice or bad.

1 Listen. Are these sounds nice or bad? Draw the symbols.

☺ nice ☹ bad

2 Give more examples of nice sounds.

LONG AND SHORT SOUNDS

Sounds can be long or short.

1 **Are these sounds long or short? Listen and circle.**

long —— short —

a

b

c

2 **Make a sound like an ambulance. Is it long or short?**

We measure music in **beats**. You can tap the beat with your finger.

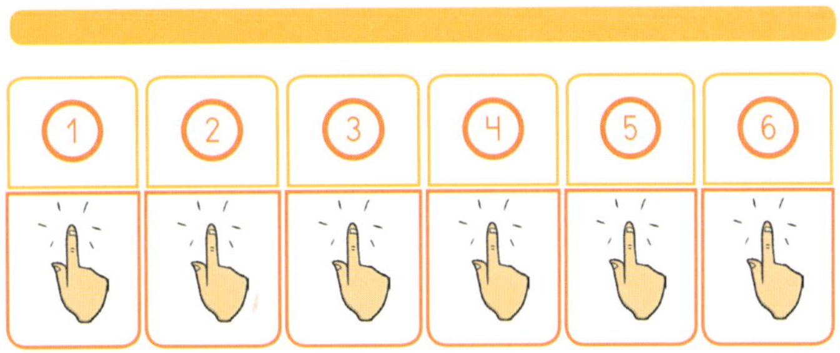

This sound lasts six beats.

1 Listen, sing and tap. Write the numbers.

1 ah

2 eh

3 oh

2 Make a sound. How many beats does it last?

Play

BODY PERCUSSION

Our body can be a musical instrument. Each part of the body can make a different sound.

1 **Copy these rhythms.**

a

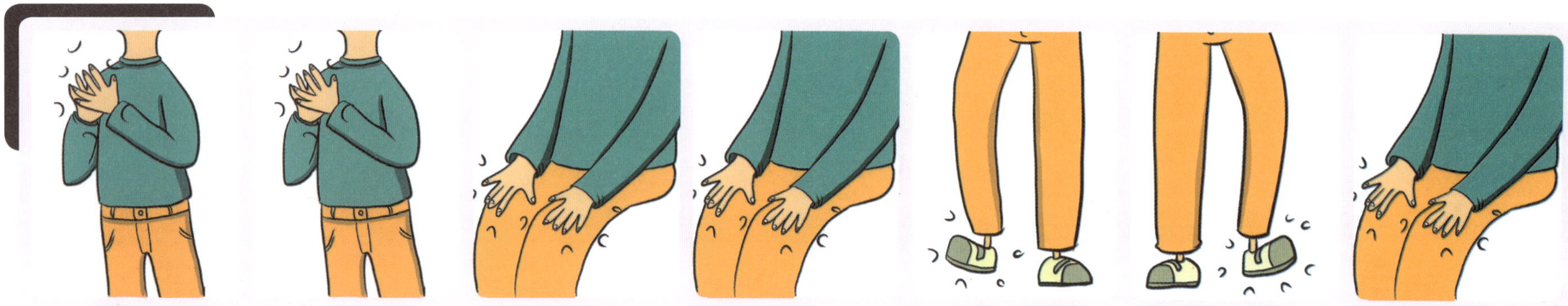

b

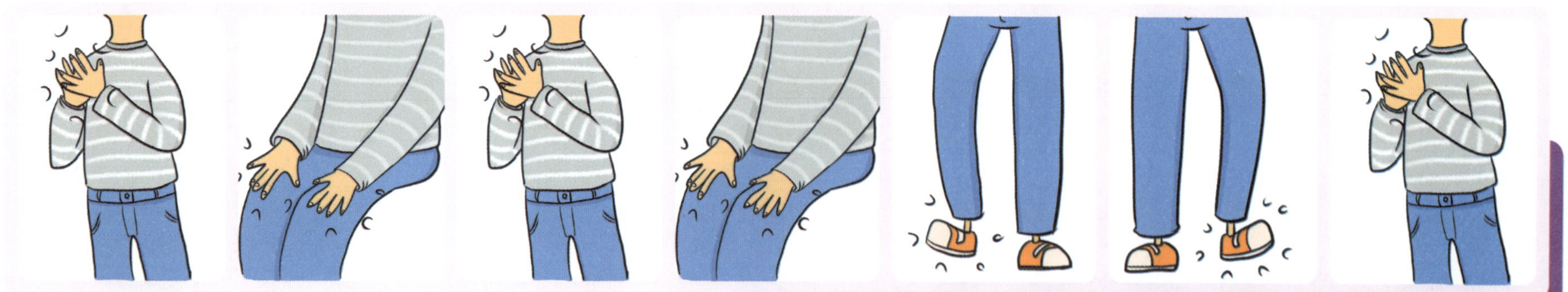

2 **Invent a rhythm using different parts of your body.**

3 **Listen. Do the actions.**

Sing

OUR VOICE

Our **voice** is an instrument. We can use it to make music.

1 **Read the words. Follow the beat with your finger.**

We sing	tah-cah	tah-cah	tah-cah	tah-cah	tah-cah	tah.	
1	2	3	4	5	6	7	8

We sing	tah-cah	tah.		Ha-ha	ha-ha	ha.	
1	2	3	4	5	6	7	8

4 **2** **Listen and sing.**

IN MY KITCHEN

1 **Look at the pictures. Do the actions.**

a

Walk in circles.

b

Clap your hands.
Stamp your feet.

c

Mime playing an instrument.

6 **2** **Listen and dance.**

TALK ABOUT MUSIC

1 Listen. Read and complete.

a 

This sound is long and nice.

b 

This sound is ______ and ______.

c 

This sound is ______ and ______.

d 

This sound is ______ and ______.

2 Listen and match. Talk about these sounds.

sound 1 •

• 

sound 2 •

• 

3 Invent a rhythm. Give instructions to your classmate.

- Stamp your feet.
- Pat your legs.
- Clap your hands.

2 SONGS AT SCHOOL

7 **Listen and sing.**

Shh!

Ta, ta, shh! In our music class.
Ta, ta, shh! Our teacher says.
Ta, ta, shh! 'Please, listen to me,
in our music class today.'

...

p. 65

1 **Circle the musical instruments.**

2 **Who is a bit worried? Point.**

3 **What light and dark colours can you see?**

Listen

LOUD AND SOFT SOUNDS

Sounds can be **loud** or **soft**.

1 Listen and number the sounds. Colour in the circles.

loud   soft

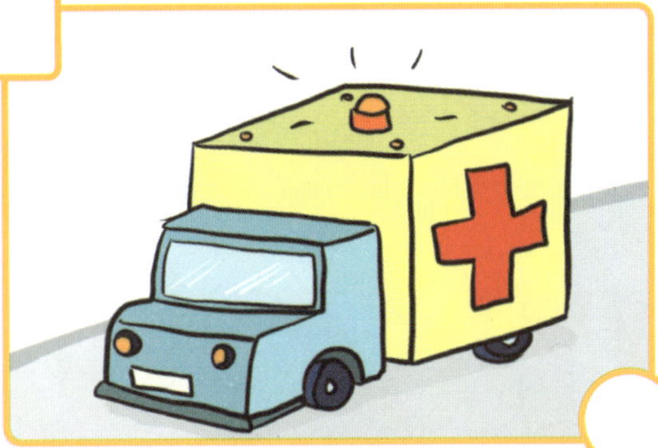

1

Discover

ONE BEAT - TA

Some sounds last one beat.
We call these sounds ta.

ta
1

1 Listen and tap.

ta	ta	ta	ta
1	2	3	4

2 Copy the rhythm.

ta	ta	ta	ta

Discover

SOUNDS AND SILENCES

Music contains sounds and silences. **Silence** is when there is no sound.

1 Listen and colour.

sound   silence

a   b   c

2 Tap the rhythm.

ta	ta	ta		ta	ta	ta	
1	2	3	4	5	6	7	8

Play

FEEL THE RHYTHM

1 Copy the rhythm. Use different parts of your body.

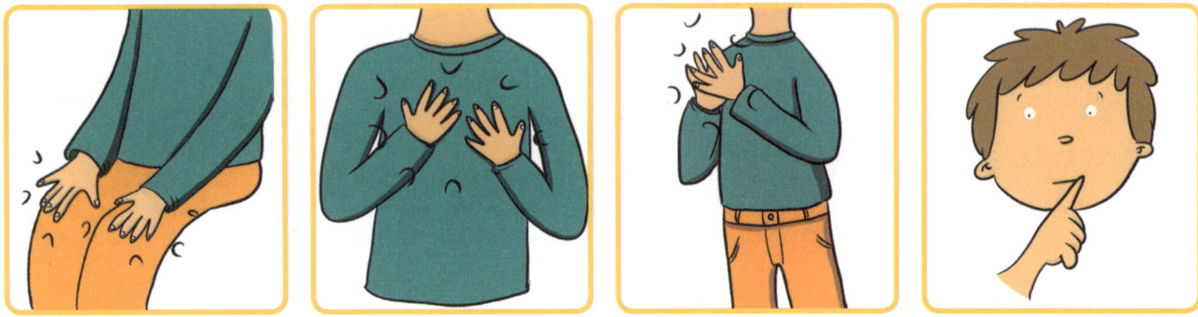

2 Work with your classmates. Play the rhythms.

a

b

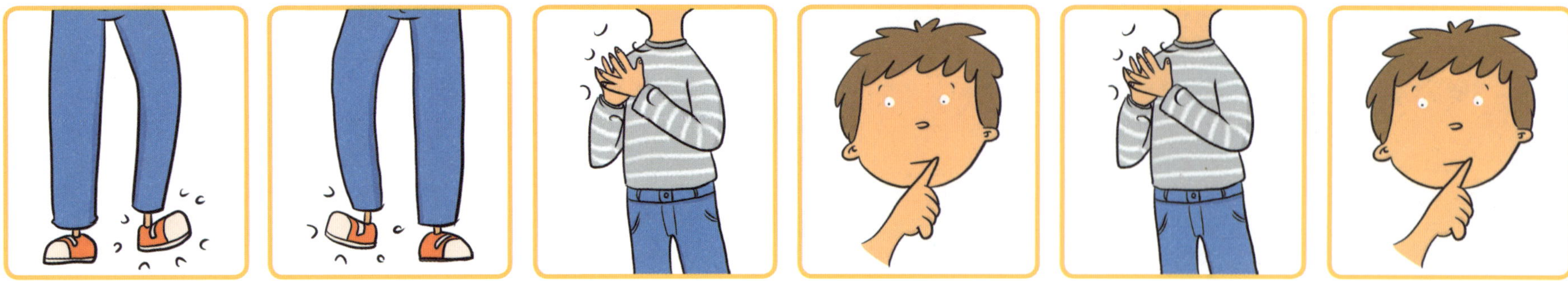

3 Invent and play a rhythm.

Sing

PARTS OF A SONG

Songs have different parts.

- The **chorus** is the part that repeats.
- The **verses** are the parts that change.

9 1 Sing the *Yummy, yummy food* song.

Chorus

Yummy, yummy food!
What is your favourite food?
Yummy, yummy food!
What is your favourite food?

Verse 1

I like sausages,
broccoli and cheese.
I like sausages,
broccoli and peas.

Chorus

Yummy, yummy food!
What is your favourite food?
Yummy, yummy food!
What is your favourite food?

Verse 2

I like chocolate,
tomatoes and ham.
I like chocolate,
tomatoes and jam.

Create

HAWAIIAN RHYTHM STICKS

Make rhythm sticks using cardboard rolls.

1 Find two long cardboard rolls, scissors and duct tape.

2 Cut slits on one side of the cardboard rolls.

3 Wrap the other ends in duct tape. Decorate your rhythm sticks.

4 Play your rhythm sticks.

MATERIALS

- 2 long cardboard rolls
- duct tape
- felt tips
- scissors

5 Work with your classmates. Invent a rhythm using your rhythm sticks and different parts of your body.

TALK ABOUT MUSIC

1 Listen. Write loud or soft.

a 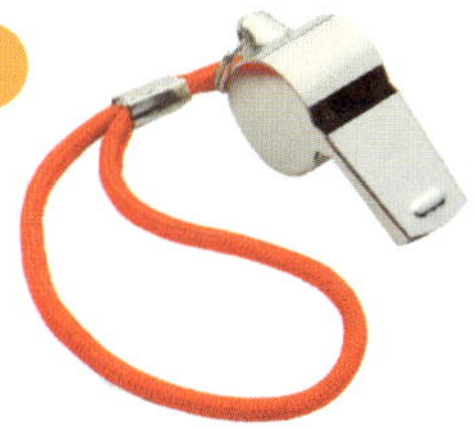
This sound is loud.

b 
This sound is ______.

c 
This sound is ______.

d 
This sound is ______.

e 
This sound is ______.

2 Match.

Verses •	• repeats.
A chorus •	• change.

3 Talk about your favourite song.

- What is the title?
  The title is ...
- How many verses does it have?
  It has ...
- How does the chorus go?

3 STREET BEATS

11 Listen and sing.

In the street

Children playing, cars stopping,
people walking in the street.
Children playing, cars stopping.
Yeah! Listen to the beat!

...

p. 66

1 Circle the things that make loud sounds.

2 Point to the living things.

3 What shapes can you see?

Listen

HIGH AND LOW SOUNDS

Sounds can be **high** or **low**.

1 **Match the sounds and pictures. Write high or low.**

sound 1 | sound 2 | sound 3 | sound 4

a

b

c

low

d

Discover

REPEAT WITH ME

This symbol tells us to repeat the sounds.

1 Read and tap.

a

ta	ta	ta	
1	2	3	4

b

ta	ta		ta
1	2	3	4

2 Listen. Draw the sound symbols and write ta.

a

1	2	3	4

b

1	2	3	4

Discover

CREATE YOUR RHYTHM

1 Listen and write the rhythms your teacher plays. Tap.

a

1	2	3	4

b

1	2	3	4

2 Play the rhythms again. Use another part of the body.

3 Invent a rhythm with sounds and silences. Tap it!

a

1	2	3	4

b

1	2	3	4

Play

WOODEN PERCUSSION

We hit or shake **percussion instruments**. Some percussion instruments are made of **wood**:

claves

wood block

castanets

maracas

1 Listen and number the sounds.

☐

☐

☐

Sing

BREATHING

When we sing, it is important to pause and breathe.

1 **Read slowly. Focus on your breathing.**

I like singing with my classmates.
Music class is fun.

13 **2** **Listen to the song and sing it with your classmates.**

With my father, father, father
and my mother, mother, mother,
we go to the beach together,
in the sunny, sunny weather.
With my sister, sister, sister
and my brother, brother, brother,
we go to the beach together,
in the sunny, sunny weather.

IN THE STREET

Dances have different parts. Each part has different **steps**.

14 1 **Look, listen and dance.**

Walk forwards.
Walk backwards.

Walk in a circle.

Do-si-do with a partner.

TALK ABOUT MUSIC

1 Listen and match.

sound 1	maracas
sound 2	claves
sound 3	castanets
sound 4	wood block

2 Listen. Talk about sounds.

a. This sound is **high** / **low**.

b. This sound is ...

c. This sound is ...

3 Ask your classmate.

a. Is a trumpet a percussion instrument?

- [ ] Yes, it is.
- [ ] No, it isn't.

b. Is a wood block a percussion instrument?

- [ ] Yes, it is.
- [ ] No, it isn't.

c. Are claves percussion instruments?

- [ ] Yes, they are.
- [ ] No, they aren't.

4 SHOP AND SING

15 Listen and sing.

Shopping rap

I am at the shopping centre,
I dance with my friend.
I am at the shopping centre,
I rap with my friend. p. 67
...

1 Count the children.

2 Circle the clothes shop.

3 What primary colours can you see?

Listen

TIMBRE

Instruments and voices have different **timbres**.

1 Listen and number the pictures.

1

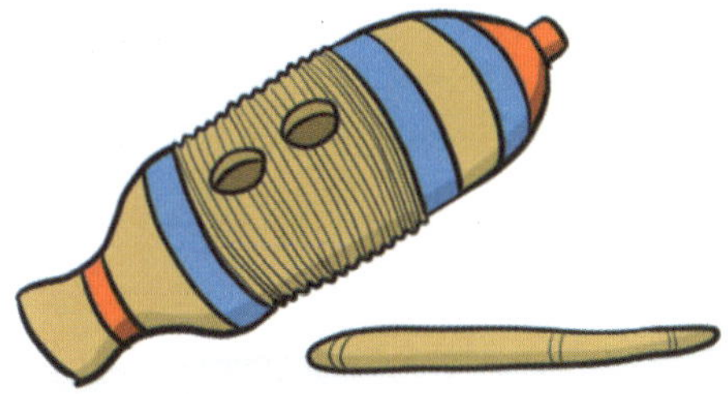

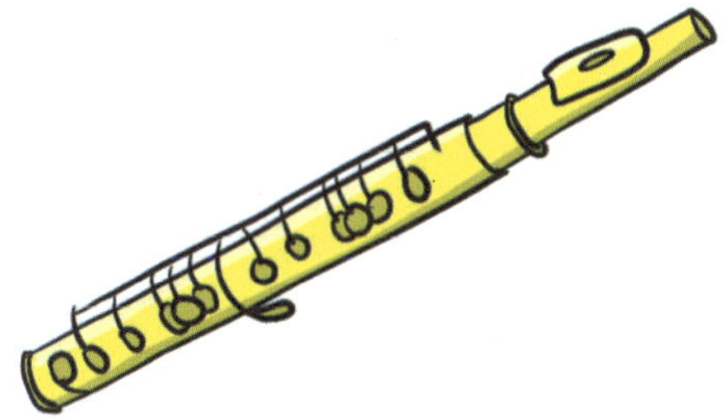

Discover

TI TI

Some sounds last half a beat.
They are called **ti ti**.

ti ti

REMEMBER

Notes that last one beat are called **ta**.

ta

1 Write **ta** or **ti ti**. Listen and play the rhythms.

a

ti ti			
1	2	3	4

b

ta		ta		ti ti		ta	
1	2	3	4	5	6	7	8

Discover

WHAT SOUNDS DO THEY MAKE?

Some words sound like people, animals or things.

1 Match.

baa!

woof!

ding dong!

17 **2** Read aloud and sing.

Woof, woof, woof, woof, woof goes the dog. (x2)
Baa, baa, baa, baa, baa goes the sheep. (x2)
La, la, la, la, la, la, la, la. (x2)

Play

METAL PERCUSSION

We hit or shake **metal percussion instruments**.

triangle

bells

cymbals

1 **Listen and number the instruments. Write.**

a

b

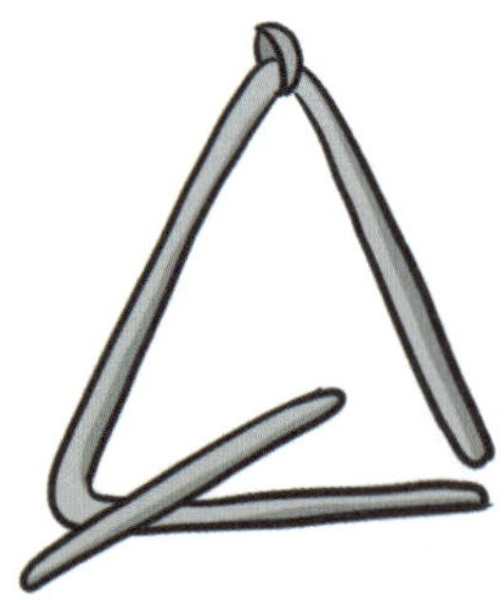

c

Sing

WHO'S SINGING?

There are **male** voices, **female** voices and **children's** voices.

1 Listen and match.

sound 1	sound 2	sound 3
child	male	female

19 2 Listen to the song *Big eyes* and number the voices. Sing.

a ☐

b ☐

c ☐

Big eyes

In the night you
hear me singing,
I have feathers and
big eyes.
In the night you
hear me singing.
Do you know I'm
very wise?

Create

MARACAS

Make maracas using recycled materials.

1 Find a can, a pot and a cardboard box.

2 Put some rice in the can.

3 Tape the can shut with sticky tape.

4 Shake your maraca.

MATERIALS

- a drink can
- a yoghurt pot
- a cardboard box
- rice
- sticky tape

5 Repeat steps 2 to 4 with the pot and the box.

6 Compare the sounds of the three maracas. Play a rhythm.

TALK ABOUT MUSIC

1 **Read and complete.**

a 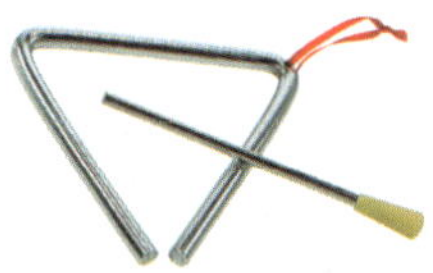 The triangle is made of metal.

b  Maracas are made of wood.

c  Bells are made of ______.

d 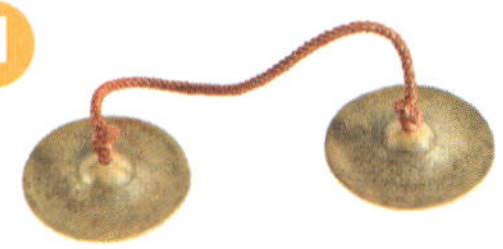 Cymbals are made of ______.

e  Claves are made of ______.

f  Castanets are made of ______.

2 **Talk about your favorite percussion instruments.**

- My favourite percussion instruments are the ... and the ...
- They are made of ...
- We hit / shake the ...
- We hit / shake the ...

3 **Ask a classmate.**

What percussion instruments can you play?

5 MUSICAL LANDSCAPES

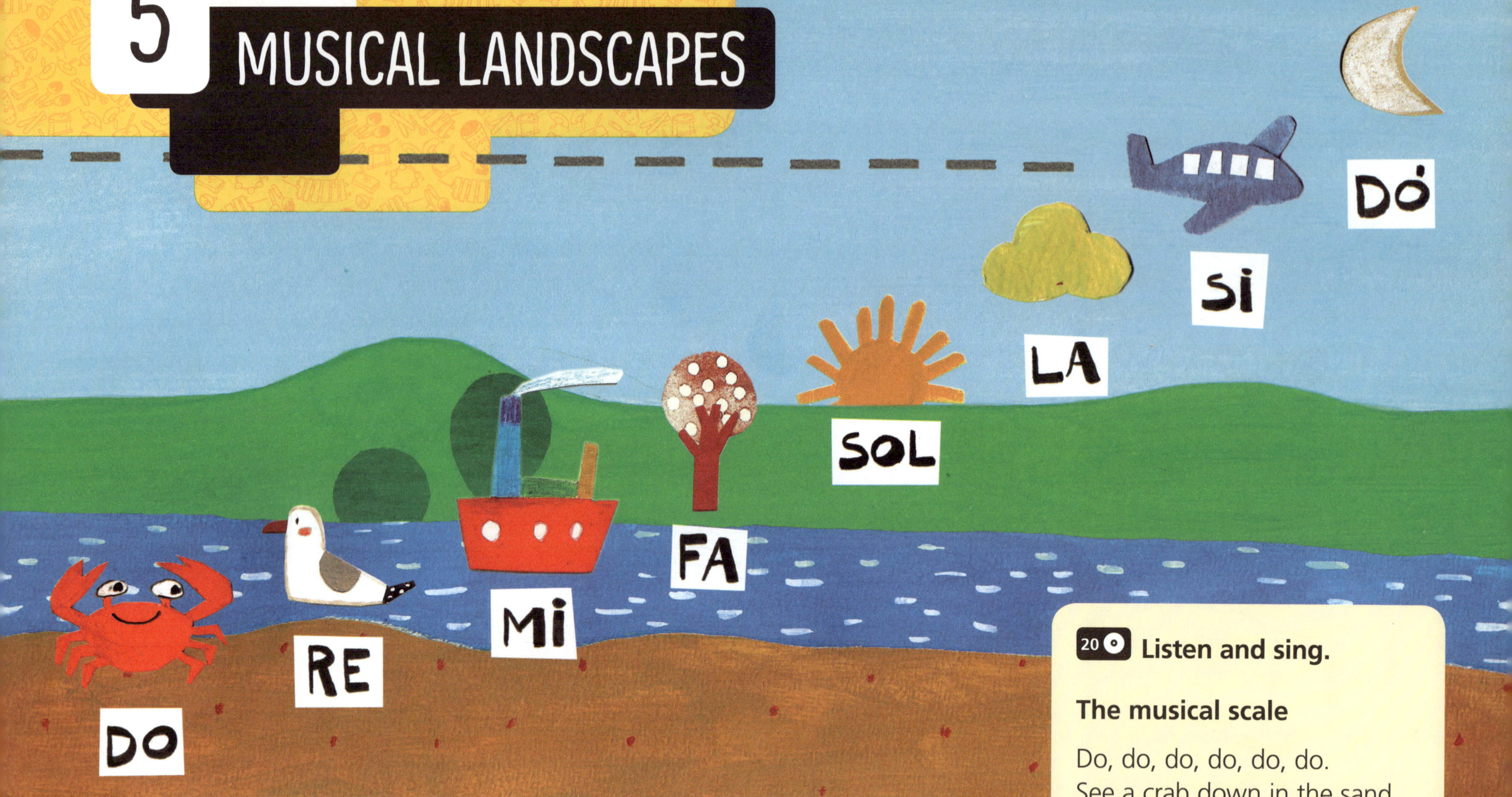

1 Circle the living things.

2 Name the objects in the musical scale.

3 What warm and cool colours can you see?

20 **Listen and sing.**

The musical scale

Do, do, do, do, do, do.
See a crab down in the sand
beneath the sea.

p. 68

Do, do, do, do, do, do, do, do,
do, do, do, do, do, do, do, do.
Can you see?
...

Listen

NATURAL AND ARTIFICIAL SOUNDS

Sounds can be natural or artificial. **Natural sounds** come from nature. Objects made by humans make **artificial sounds**.

1 Listen and match. Write natural or artificial.

sound 1

sound 2

sound 3

Discover
TA-A

Some sounds last two beats. We call these sounds **ta-a**.

ta-	a

This symbol means that the note lasts two beats.

REMEMBER

ta	=	ta
ti ti	=	ti ti

1 Listen and tap.

ta	ti ti	ta-	a	ta	ti ti	ta-	a

2 Invent a rhythm. Use ta, ti ti and ta-a. Clap the rhythm.

Discover

NOTES DO, RE AND MI

A **note** is how high or low a sound is. **Do**/C, **re**/D and **mi**/E are notes in the musical scale. **Do** and **mi** are always on a line. **Re** is always in the space between them.

1 Listen and sing.

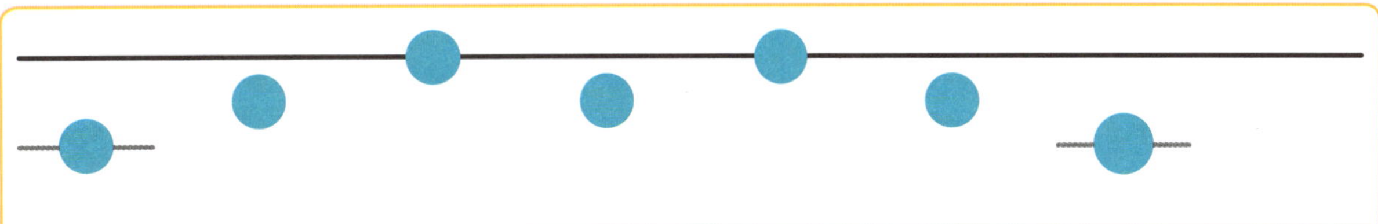

do	re	mi	re	mi	re	do	

2 Read, sing and write.

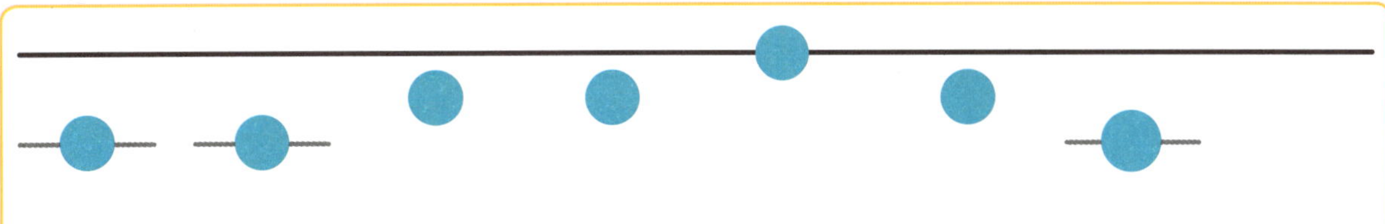

do							

Play

DRUMS AND MORE

Some instruments have skins. We hit some using our hands and others using drumsticks.

drum

tambourine

bass drum

1 Listen, number and write the instruments.

a

b

c

Sing

MUSICAL SCALE

1 Sing and touch each note.

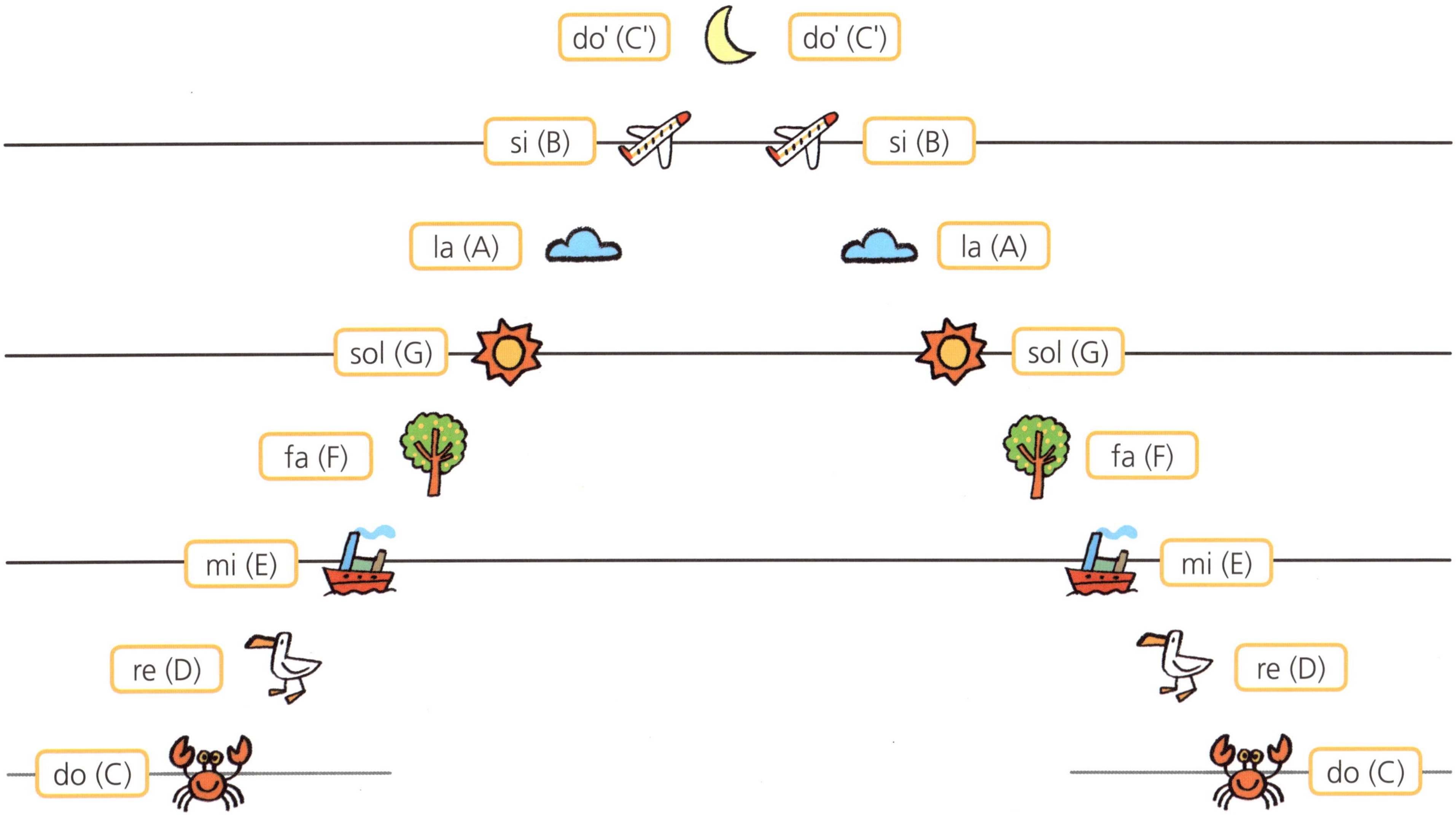

2 Sing the scale like an animal.

THE PRETTY FLOWER DANCE

23 **1** **Look, listen and dance.**

Verse 1

Spin with a partner.

Chorus

Clap hands with
a partner.

Verse 2

Point your right foot.
Point your left foot.

Verse 3

Touch elbows with
a partner.

TALK ABOUT MUSIC

1 Listen. Write natural or artificial.

a ____________________

b ____________________

c ____________________

d ____________________

2 Ask your classmate.

a. Can you play the drum?

☐ Yes, I can. ☐ No, I can't.

b. Can you play the bass drum?

☐ Yes, I can. ☐ No, I can't.

c. Can you play the tambourine?

☐ Yes, I can. ☐ No, I can't.

3 Look at the pictures. Talk about sounds. Use the words below.

The **dog** makes a loud **sound**.

- nice
- bad
- soft
- loud
- long
- short
- artificial
- natural

a

b

c

d

6 SHOWTIME!

24 **Listen and sing.**

I love the circus

Circus! I love the circus.
I love the circus,
it is here for you and me.

Listen! I hear the music.
I hear the music,
playing just for you and me.

...

p. 69

1. **Circle the musicians.**
2. **Who is wearing a hat?**
3. **Point to the background.**

Listen

VOLUME AND SPEED

Music can be loud or soft and fast or slow.

26 **1** **Listen. Pay attention to the change of volume and speed.**

26 **2** **Listen again. How does this music make you feel?**

Discover

NOTES FA AND SOL

The note **fa**/F is in a space.
The note **sol**/G is on a line.

REMEMBER

- half beat
- one beat
- two beats

1 Listen and tap.

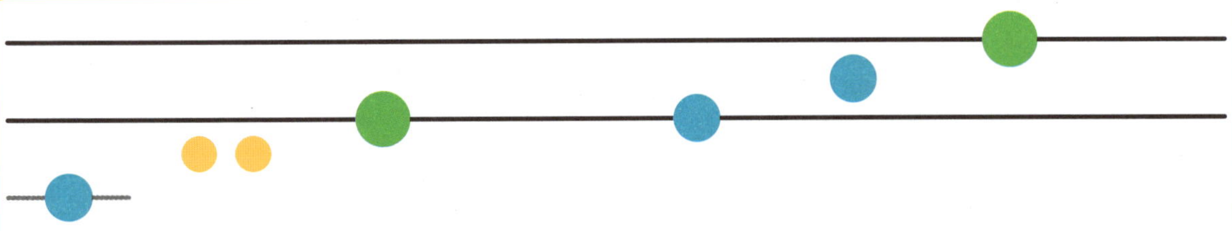

do	re re	mi		mi	fa	sol	

2 Read, sing and write.

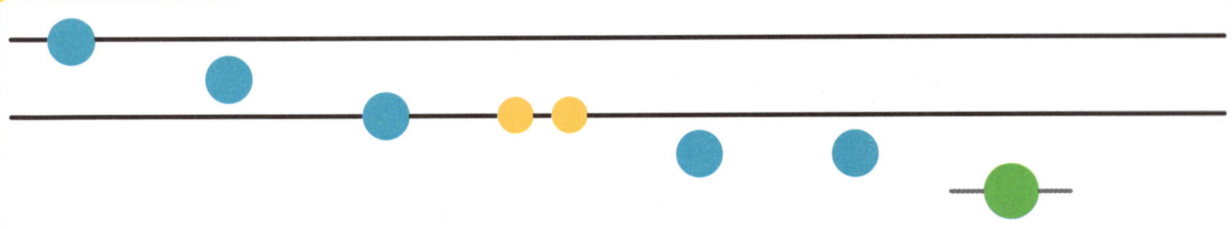

sol							

THE STAVE AND TREBLE CLEF

We write music notes on the **stave**. It has five lines with four spaces. We write the **treble clef** at the start.

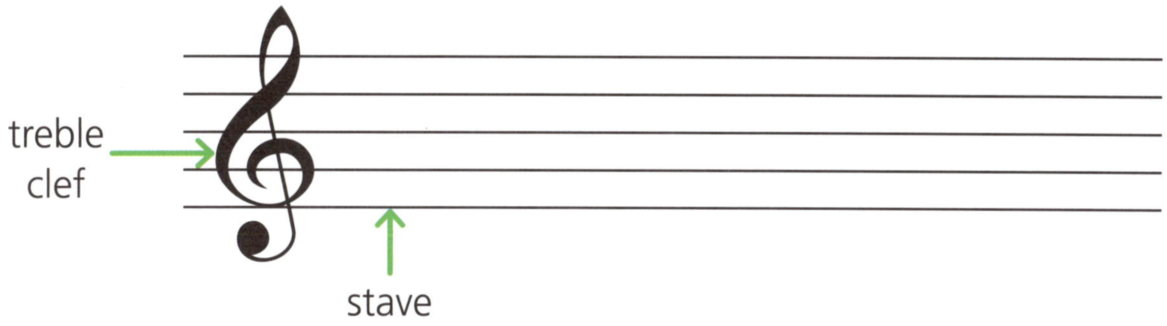

1 **Trace over the treble clefs. Start from the dot.**

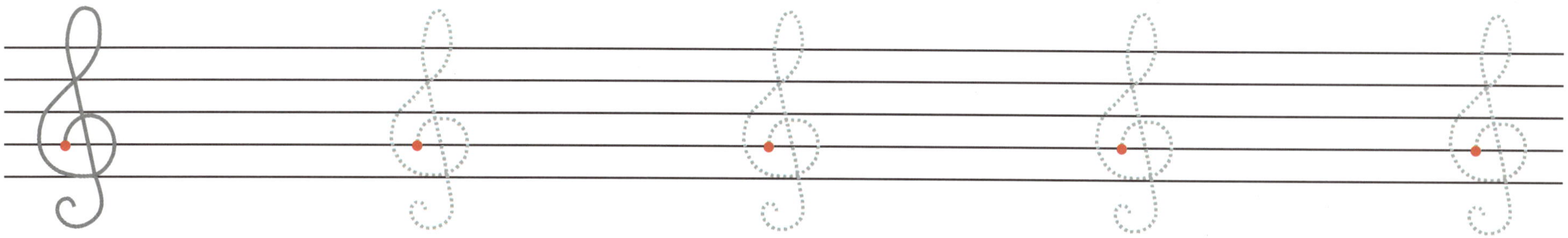

2 **Draw treble clefs.**

Play

PLAYING WITH RHYTHM

A rhythm is a repeated musical idea.

1 Listen to the rhythms your teacher plays. Play.

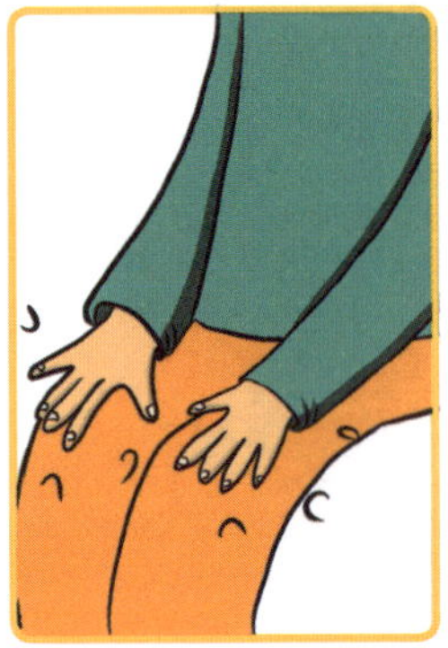

ta		ta	

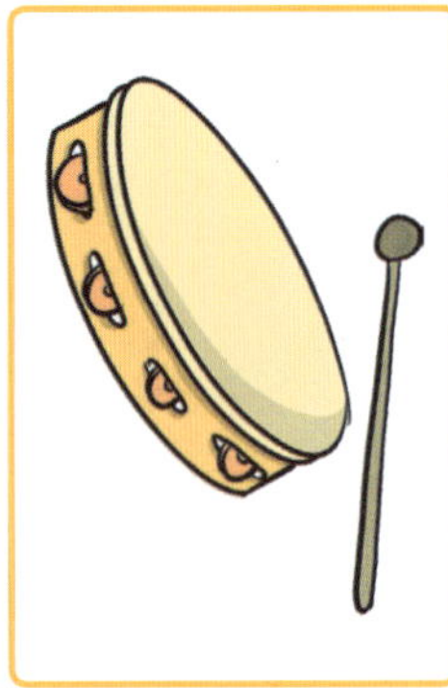

ta		ti ti	ta

ta	ta	ta	ta

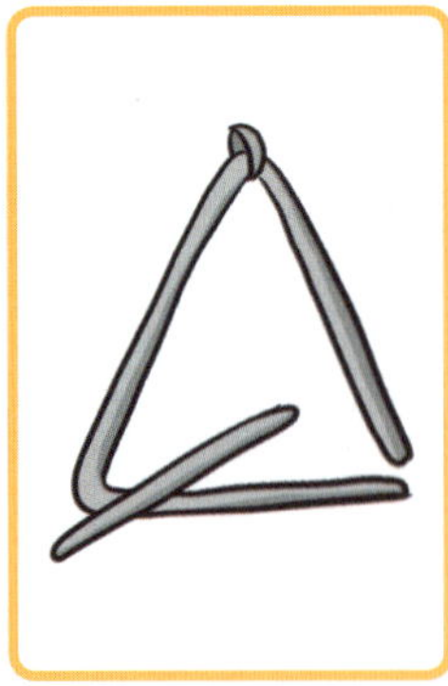

ta			

2 What do you prefer, the triangle or tambourine?

Sing

FOLLOW THE ROBOT

27 1 **Sing the *Follow the robot* song.**

Follow, follow the robot,
with metal arms and metal legs.
Follow, follow the robot,
with metal hands and a metal head. (x2)

Come on robot! Move your arms!
Beep, beep, beep, beep, boop, boop, boop.

Follow, follow the robot,
with metal arms and metal legs.
Follow, follow the robot,
with metal hands and a metal head. (x2)

Come on robot! Move your legs!
Beep, beep, beep, beep, boop, boop, boop.

La, la, la, la, la, la, la, la.
La, la, la, la, la, la, la.
La, la, la, la, la, la, la, la.
La, la, la, la, la, la, la.

Come on all the robots! Come on!

27 2 **Sing the song again. Move with the music.**

Create

A CONCERT PROGRAMME

A **concert programme** gives us information about a concert.

The **composer** writes music.

The **conductor** directs the musicians.

Each **musician** plays a different instrument.

1 Match.

musician	composer	conductor
Composes a piece of music.	Directs an orchestra.	Plays an instrument.

2 Make a concert programme with your classmates.

TALK ABOUT MUSIC

1 **Read and complete.**

a. A composer writes music.

b. A ______________ plays musical instruments.

c. A ______________ directs musicians in an orchestra.

2 **Write the notes.**

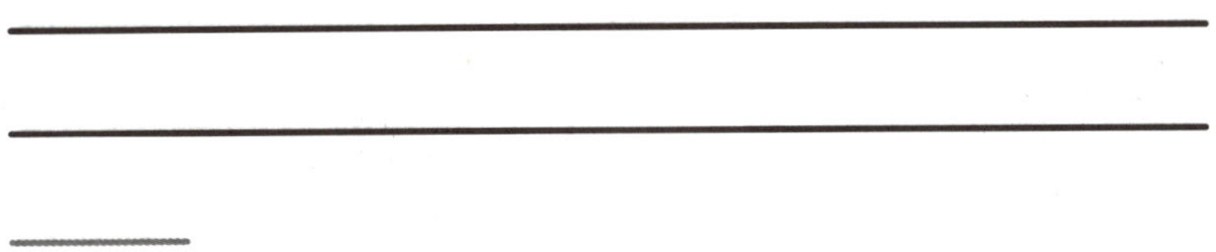

do re mi fa sol

3 **Talk about your concert programme.**

- What is the title of the concert?
- What is the name of the orchestra?
- Who is the composer?
- Who is the conductor?
- Who are the musicians? What instruments do they play?
- When is the concert?
- Where is the concert?

LISTENING TO MUSIC

1 Which objects play music? Circle.

2 Trace.

a

stereo

b

MP3 player

c

headphones

HOW DO WE COMMUNICATE?

1 Work in groups. Tick (✓) the correct behaviour.

a ☐

b ☐

c ☐

2 Work in groups. Make a string phone. Talk to a classmate.

1. Punch a hole at the bottom of each cup.
2. Pass the string through each cup.
3. Tie knots at each end.

MATERIALS

- 2 plastic cups
- nail (adult supervision required)
- string

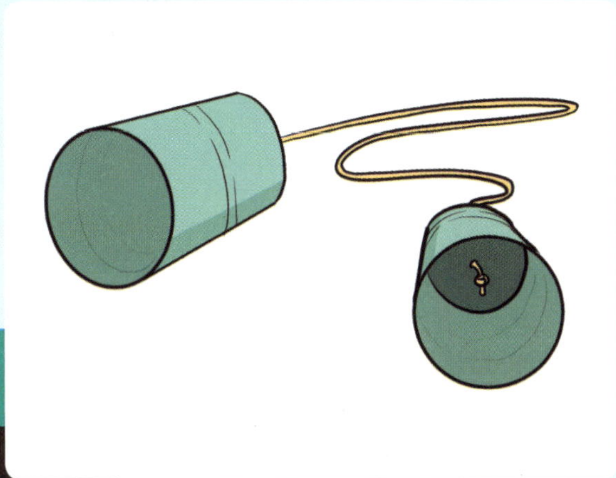

MUSIC AROUND US

1 Which objects play music? Look and colour.

2 Colour the objects.

laptop — tablet — speakers

a

b

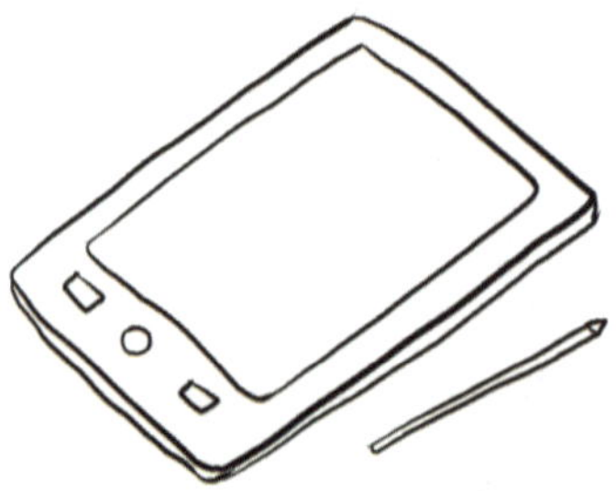

c

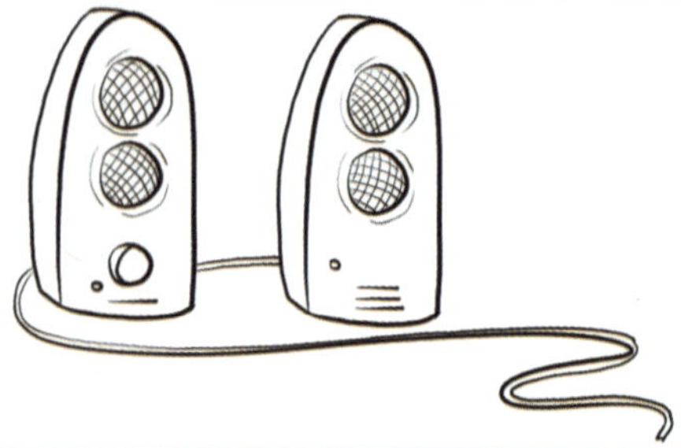

LISTEN SAFELY AND RESPONSIBLY

1 **Work in groups. Tick (✓) the correct behaviour.**

a ☐

b ☐

c ☐

2 **What are the rules for safe and responsible listening? Make a poster.**

1. Work in groups.
2. Use pictures.
3. Use texts.

MATERIALS

- coloured card
- coloured pencils
- crayons
- felt tips
- glue stick
- scissors

PLAYING MUSIC

1 Which object plays music? Tick (✓).

a ☐

b ☐

c ☐

2 Match.

a

b

c

d

smartphone

MP3 player

tablet

laptop

FEEL THE MUSIC

1 Listen. Draw how you feel.

a

b

c

d

29 2 Work in groups. How does this piece of music make you feel? Make a collage.

- Listen to *Morning mood* by Edvard Grieg.
- Act out how you feel.
- Use images to illustrate your feelings.

MATERIALS

- glue stick
- photos
- scissors

FESTIVALS

Term 1

CHRISTMAS IS HERE!

30 1 **Listen and clap your hands. Sing.**

Christmas is here,
Christmas is here,
the snow is on the ground.
We play a song,
we play a song,
when Santa comes to town.

Clap your hands.
Play the horn.
Stamp your feet.
Bang the drum.

Repeat chorus

Shake the bells.
Play the trumpet.
Slide the trombone.
Let's sing, come on!

Repeat chorus

30 2 Listen and act.

30 3 Listen. Copy the rhythm.

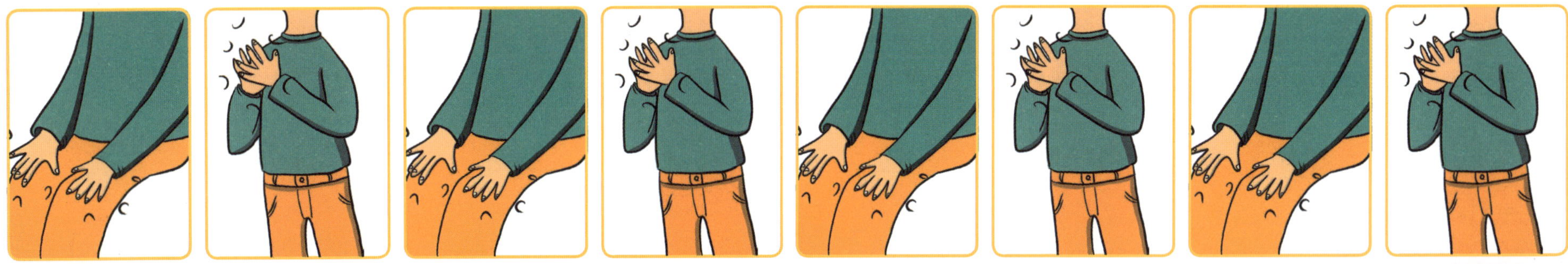

30 4 Work in groups.

group 1: Mark the beat using parts of your body.
group 2: Mime playing the instruments from the song.

FESTIVALS

Term 2

THE EASTER BUNNY

32 **1 Listen and clap the beat. Sing.**

The Easter bunny is very funny,
spring is here today.
The Easter bunny is very funny.
Hip, hip, hip, hooray!

Flowers and trees,
birds and bees,
the Easter bunny plays.
Flowers and trees,
birds and bees,
sing and dance in May.

Repeat chorus

Delicious fruit,
and pretty butterflies,
the Easter bunny plays.
Delicious fruit,
and pretty butterflies,
sing and dance in May.

Repeat chorus

Oh, spring is here to stay!

32 2 Work in groups. Listen. Play instruments.

group 1

group 2

group 3

33 3 Listen. Dance.

a

b

c

FESTIVALS

Term 3

SUMMER IS HERE!

34 **1 Listen and sing.**

Our last day
of school is done.
Say goodbye to all our friends.
Pack our bags.
We're going away
to spend some time on holiday.

Summer is here,
summer is nice.
Drink lemonade or juice with ice,
play some sport
or swim in the sea.
Eat fresh fruit with ice cream!

Catch a train
or fly on a plane.
Travelling can be fun.
Take your toys
meet girls and boys
and play under the sun.

Repeat chorus

34 **2** **Sing and act.**

34 **3** **Work in groups. Listen. Play instruments.**

group 1	group 2	group 3	group 4

Unit 1 2

In my kitchen

In my kitchen, in my kitchen,
in my kitchen, I hear sounds.
In my kitchen, in my kitchen,
in my kitchen, I hear sounds.

In my kitchen I hear sounds.
They make music.
Music!

In my kitchen I hear sounds.
They make music.
Music!

I hear the clock on the wall –
ticking.
I hear the white microwave –
beeping.
I hear the hot water – bubbling.
I hear the red telephone – ringing.

Shh!

Ta, ta, shh! In our music class.
Ta, ta, shh! Our teacher says.
Ta, ta, shh! 'Please listen to me,
in our music class today'.

Beats, short and long sounds
and rhythms.
Music class is fun.
Beats, short and long sounds
and rhythms.
Ta, ta, ta, ta, ta, come on!

Ta, ta, shh! In our music (silence).
Ta, ta, shh! Our teacher (silence).
Ta, ta, shh! 'Please listen
(silence),
in our music class today'.

Beats, short and long sounds
and rhythms.
Music class is fun.
Beats, short and long sounds
and rhythms.
Ta, ta, ta, ta, ta, come on!

Ta, ta, shh! In our (silence).
Ta, ta, shh! The (silence).
Ta, ta, shh! 'Please (silence),
in our music class today'.

SONG LYRICS

Unit 3 11

In the street

I am in the street today
with grandad.
I am in the street today
with my dog.
We hear sounds – loud
and soft in the street.
Hear the sounds and listen
to the beat.

Children playing, cars stopping,
people walking in the street.
Children playing, cars stopping.
Yeah! Listen to the beat!

Listen, listen to the beat!
Loud and soft sounds in the street.
Listen, listen to the beat!
What can you hear in the street?

Repeat chorus

Unit 4 15

Shopping rap

I am at the shopping centre,
I dance with my friend.
I am at the shopping centre,
I rap with my friend.

I am at the shopping centre,
I sing with my friend.
I am at the shopping centre,
I rap with my friend.

I am at the shopping centre,
I dance with my friend.
I am at the shopping centre,
I rap with my friend.

I am at the shopping centre,
I sing with my friend.
I am at the shopping centre,
I rap with my friend.

Ra-a-a-a-a-ping!
Sho-o-o-o-o-ping!
Play-ay-ay-ay-ay-ing!
Sing-ing-ing-ing-ing-ing!
Oh! Yeah! Oh! Yeah!

Rapping at the shopping centre,
wo-oh, oh!
Rapping at the shopping centre,
yeah, yeah, yeah!

SONG LYRICS

Unit 5 20

The musical scale

Do, do, do, do, do, do.
See a crab down in the sand beneath the sea.

Do, do, do, do, do, do, do, do,
do, do, do, do, do, do, do, do.
Can you see?

Re, re, re, re, re, re.
See a bird playing and swimming, can you see?

Mi, mi, mi, mi, mi.
See a boat sailing on the sea.

Fa, fa, fa, fa, fa.
See a tree on the land so far.

Sol, sol, sol, sol, sol, sol.
See the Sun shining on us all.

La, la, la, la, la, la.
See a cloud above the land.

Si, si, si, si.
See a plane drawing a line.
Oh! Can you see?

Do, do, do, do, do.
See the Moon shining on the sea.

In the ... musical scale for you and me.

Unit 6 24

I love the circus

Circus! I love the circus.
I love the circus,
it is here for you and me.

Listen! I hear the music.
I hear the music,
playing just for you and me.

Repeat chorus

Listen! I hear performers.
I hear performers,
waiting to entertain you and me.

Repeat chorus

La, la, la, la, la, la, la,
la, la, la, la, la, la,
la, la, la, la, la, la.

PICTURE DICTIONARY

Sounds

long

short

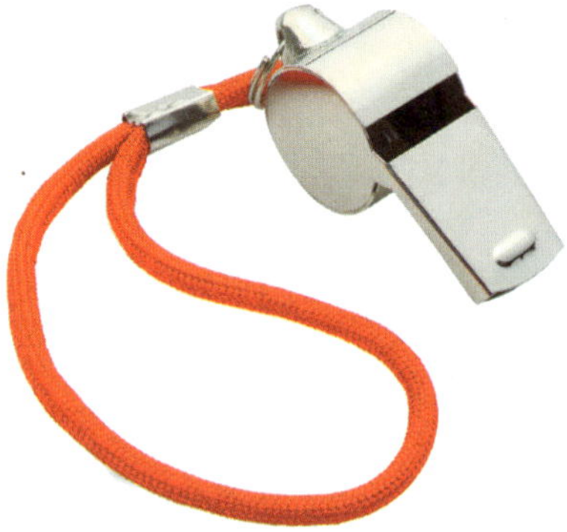

loud

soft

high

low

natural

artificial

Wooden percussion instruments

wood block

claves

castanets

maracas

Metal percussion instruments

triangle

bells

cymbals

Drums and more

drum

tambourine

bass drum

CD TRACKS

TRACK	SONG
01	Introduction
02	In my kitchen
03	In my kitchen (instrumental)
04	Tah-cah-tah
05	Tah-cah-tah (instrumental)
06	In my kitchen (dance)
07	Shh!
08	Shh! (instrumental)
09	Yummy, yummy food
10	Yummy, yummy food (instrumental)
11	In the street
12	In the street (instrumental)
13	We go to the beach together
14	In the street (dance)
15	Shopping rap
16	Shopping rap (instrumental)
17	Animal sounds
18	Animal sounds (instrumental)
19	Big eyes
20	The musical scale
21	The musical scale (instrumental)
22	Can you plant a pretty flower?
23	Can you plant a pretty flower? (dance)
24	I love the circus
25	I love the circus (instrumental)
26	*Neapolitan Dance* from *Swan Lake*, P. I. Tchaikovsky
27	Follow the robot
28	Follow the robot (instrumental)
29	*Morning mood*, E. Grieg
30	Christmas is here!
31	Christmas is here! (instrumental)
32	The Easter bunny
33	The Easter bunny (instrumental)
34	Summer is here!
35	Summer is here! (instrumental)